Loving an Older Dog

Warm, wise writings and adv
on living with an aging pet

Loving an Older Dog

Jacqueline A. Meyers, PhD

Founder of Peaceful Passings
Senior Animal Rescue

www.mascotbooks.com

Loving an Older Dog

For more information, please contact:
Mascot Books
620 Herndon Parkway #320
Herndon, VA 20170
info@mascotbooks.com

Library of Congress Control Number: 2019900368

ISBN-13: 978-1-64307-432-0
CPSIA Code: PRTWP0419A

Printed in Malaysia

First and foremost, I want to thank my husband, Dave Sagarin, for years of help and support of our rescue. Without him, there would not have ever been a Peaceful Passings Senior Animal Rescue. Many thanks to our adopters, some of whom adopted animals in their "teens" including some who were hospice with only a short time to live. Without their love, dedication, and caring, these dogs would have passed without having known a forever home.

I want to thank those who have served on our Board of Directors, who gave of their time and expertise, to help dogs in their golden years. Without them, we could not have survived. There are our foster parents, who are always there to take on the animals needing rehabilitation, training, and a safe spot to lay their heads. Beyond this, our wonderful supporters who through the internet and social media have stood by us through thick and thin, donating their dollars and words of love and encouragement. To date, they have helped us save over 700 senior animals and I could not be more appreciative.

The animal community is one where we support each other, work hard to save another life, and truly make a difference. We could not do the work we do, fulfill our mission and vision, without their help. Our mission is to save senior animals. Our vision is a world where no animal is euthanized because of age or medical challenge when a quality of life remains. For those who understand, thank you. For those who may be new to this concept, we hope to bring you into the fold. Our goal is to inspire people to consider adopting a senior animal. Senior animal lives are worth saving.

Finally, I would like to thank my parents for giving me life.

Contents

Preface

When I started my rescue in rural Virginia, attitudes were not all animal friendly. Over time, I have witnessed a change in how people value animals as family members. This has brought me great joy and hope for the future. Advocacy for senior animals is a large part of my work. I am encouraged by the change.

A Changing Paradigm

"**I** saw those people in New Orleans and I realized that I could never let myself be rescued if it meant leaving my pets."

Hurricane Katrina brought this country a recognition of something that has been developing for a long time—a paradigm shift in the way we view our animal companions. Thomas Kuhn, author of *The Structure of Scientific Revolution* first coined the term "paradigm shift" to describe a major shift in a world view, where an accepted view is overturned by an "intellectually violent revolution" due to the occurrence of significant event(s). In our relation to animal companions, this change has come from the work of the animal rights movement and events such as Hurricane Katrina. The "shift" impacts how we perceive animals and their place in our world.

Concerns for basic animal welfare evolved into the animal rights movement, which advocates that animals are worthy of both legal and physical protection. "It's just an animal" has been replaced with a view that the human-animal bond has immense potential for great depth, which is still being defined. As the bond grows, our identification with animals becomes stronger. Animals are less likely to be objectified with names such as Fluffy or Spot, having been elevated to human names like Burt and Alice. This clearly reflects our need for establishing relationships with animals.

Hurricane Katrina was the catalyst for national legislation insuring pet owners the right to provide protection for their pets in the case of a declared disaster. This has led to similar legislation at the state level. Shelters are being established for companion pets during disasters. Owners will never be challenged with the heart wrenching decision to either evacuate leaving their pets behind or to stay with their pets while putting their own lives in peril.

Animals kept as pets were once largely regarded as property. Today, they are regarded as family members. The human-animal bond has raised our regard for animals to a place where humans and animals are mutual companions. Our goal, as humans, is no longer to dominate another species, but rather to coexist.

Animals were once valued for their economic value, as working, or service animals. "Maintaining" animals meant providing necessities: a bowl of food, water, and shelter. Today, animals possess social value. More people are providing for pets physically, medically, and psychologically, much as they do for themselves. Animals have evolved from a position of economic value, to that of being more broadly valued, as shown by the time, money and effort that humans will invest in their pets.

Specialized care and advancements in veterinary medicine have developed to address the physical and emotional issues of senior and dying animals. This is because of the paradigm shift. For example, animals, once they had passed, were replaceable with another, "substitute" puppy or kitten. Now, people realize that animals cannot be "replaced," although other animals, unique in their own personalities, can be adopted. Animals are not alike; a dog is not just like another dog; a cat is not just like another cat. Thankfully, more and more humans are coming to this realization. All of this points to a validation of the Great Spirit that animals possess, as beings, with their own value and worth.

Introduction

Grow old along with me!
The best is yet to be,
The last of life, for which the first was made ...

"Rabbi Ben Ezra" by Robert Browning

I have written this book to honor the aging process of our animal companions. It is a tribute to those people who are willing to see past puppyhood and early maturity for the rewards of sharing their lives with an older animal. It is a book about loving the imperfect and the gradual signs of aging that are inevitably shared by humans and animals. It acknowledges that all stages of life, including death, are sacred.

This book is about senior and hospice animals; those who have found their humans and those who are still waiting for that opportunity. It illustrates many of the issues that senior animals face due to their natural aging process: deemed unadoptable, rejected, and misunderstood. It speaks to the need for hospice services as an animal reaches the final passage.

Our consciousness is raised as our view of human-animal bonds broadens. Animals will inevitably age. And there are older animals languishing in shelters. Their lives will be made richer if we're able to take them into our homes. This book is about how *your* life can also be richer living with an older pet. The themes presented in the book apply to all companion animals

Urban and suburban lifestyles no longer require humans to have animals primarily for utilitarian purposes. Dogs and cats still function in traditional roles such as hunting, guarding, herding, and as therapy animals. The basis of the human-animal bond is more about relationships and less about utility. Animals are living longer and healthier lives. Better medical care is available for pets, and more people are willing to access veterinary services.

Animals as Spiritual Beings

Peaceful Passings Senior Animal Rescue is a rescue I founded as a haven for older dogs who are lost and broken. We rehabilitate, socialize, provide veterinary care, and offer a home to those who find themselves in rural shelters; a place to call home until they are adopted and if not, a permanent residence. We serve senior, hospice and special need dogs in their golden years. My learning has come from the 16 years I have offered a sanctuary for these deserving creatures. To date, my home has been shared with over 700 senior dogs.

My devotion to the well-being of animals is a calling; I can't turn away when my path crosses with an animal in need; I must try to help. In return my life is richer, because of who they are—who I experience that animal to be. My work with animals gives purpose and meaning to my life. They give me a reason for being.

I don't just give of my time and effort. I grow each time that I interact with animals. They share their distinct personalities, their past, and give me an opportunity to be part of their present. They share their energy and remind me that we are all a product of our past.

Humans are often prisoners of their past; animals actively work to grow beyond issues of neglect, abandonment, and disappointment. They are open to growing beyond the circumstances from which they came. Animals do not bemoan or resent their disabilities, physical or age-related. They accept them as part of who they are.

Animals teach us to live in the moment, to accept our past and not perseverate, or fear, what the future might bring. Animals can wait, while humans are often impatient. Many animals have waited long periods of time for their eventual rescuer to come while existing in dismal situations, not thinking about tomorrow, but focusing on the day.

Animals teach us to be compassionate, because in caring for an animal, we accept responsibility for another species. Animals teach us about relationships; each day we care for an animal builds a deeper bond with that animal. We may not be sure of what tomorrow will bring, or be secure with our current level of resources, but with an animal in our life, we will always be sure of all the wealth those relationships can bring.

We may worry about what we don't have; in the eyes of an animal companion we see everything we've got. Animals don't speak, but thankfully, they listen very closely. The closer we are to an animal, the more certain we are that we are in communication with them; we just must listen with our heart. Maybe the lesson is in how well they listen and the dialogue that allows us, as humans, to have with them internally and externally. In conversation with an animal, I own a space to verbalize my thoughts, as well as a space to think about what I've said. In those moments, my energy bonds with the animal and makes clear my eventual path. Gazing into the deep dark eyes of a canine or the prism-like eyes of a feline companion brings new ideas and inspiration. Through their eyes, I connect with a higher spiritual source.

Animals give back more than they take. When I'm sick or tired, my animals lay down next to me and I feel better, comforted and soothed. When I'm watching television, reading, or working on my computer, I feel supported and inspired. When I play my instruments, I have an audience that doesn't judge me harshly if I make mistakes. When I'm sad or discouraged, my animals console me. Every day I learn lessons about love, support, encouragement and by those lessons, I am inspired to work harder, move forward, be less fearful, more trusting, and become more that I ever imagined that I could be.

Animals are great spirits. Each animal has a completely different soul. Some are young souls who thirst for depth. Others are old souls, who have come to allow us to share the insights, those that we have yet to experience. Their purpose for being in our lives unfolds, as we come to clearly see their roles in our lives as nurse, caretaker, recreation director, bodyguard, there to bring to our lives what we need now. They possess a sense of duty, loyal to their humans and protective of their homes.

Animals are consistent. They relate in a simple, pure and direct way. They reward us with affection, with their presence, and with fun. It's easy to have a relationship with one who just loves us for who we are. The demands they make on us are simple by comparison to human relationships; a chest needing to be rubbed, a bowl of food, shelter from the elements. Animals give us total devotion in exchange for being treated humanely.

In our house, our animals, my husband and I are bound together by love. We are not just a husband and wife with pets; they are not just a pack of dogs. Together we are a family.

We live a lifestyle that may not suit everyone. We eat at mealtimes surrounded by our animals, sit with them on couch and chair, and several asleep with us in bed at night. We observe our pets closely, watching every move, mood and change. We share our achievements and our setbacks, but as a family we support and help each other to cope and move forward. The sense of family I that receive from all living beings under my roof gives me a deep sense of belonging, and in that I discover my roots.

Frida Rhea

In my experience, the animals with whom I have shared the closest bond are those who had medical issues. These are not sad stories; they are stories of courage and strength, not only for the animal but also for the human. These are the animals that I have worked most closely with and shared end of life issues. I am blessed to have shared their lives, in sickness and in health.

Frida Rhea was an eight-year-old, tri-colored female Beagle. She had problems with her intestines for about six months and had been to the vet on several occasions. Basically, the muscles of the intestines were not functioning. She was on medication to help her eliminate gas and feces. She was fed a prescription dog food mixed with a little water and mineral oil. The medication seemed to be helping. However, the vet prescribed a different medication that she thought would be more effective. When Frida bloated, she looked like she swallowed a basketball. One option was surgery to remove the colon. This could lead to diarrhea or constipation to the point where euthanasia may be the only option. We were not at that point. The vet discussed the prognosis in front of Frida

Rhea, who I believe understood what she was inferring (the possibility of euthanasia). I was not happy about that.

Frida Rhea was more independent than my other two Beagles. She loved food. I don't think she gave her illness a lot of thought. She was not ready to be euthanized. She still had much enjoyment in life. Frida Rhea lived in her own little world. She didn't care about toys but loved massages and sitting outside.

I wanted Frida to understand that I made every effort to get her the best vet and surgical team in the state of Virginia. Having achieved that, they could not tell me exactly what was wrong with her, nor what could be done about it. All their suggestions were indefinite and presented outcomes that did not represent quality of life. I did not want to let her starve to death, nor allow her to remain in a body that was painful, with organs that were not functioning correctly, and with a brain that was shutting down.

On the day she was euthanized, I heard her message: "Let's just enjoy the time we have together." I didn't want to allow her more time to enjoy her walk on a leash, because I was frantically trying to get her to the veterinary hospital, knowing that time was of the essence. I asked her to fight for herself, because I was fighting for her as best I could. Then, after we got to the animal hospital, I asked for her to accept death as freedom from her ailing body. I told her to go to the "Rainbow Bridge." Does she understand why and how I had to make that shift?

I wanted Frida to understand why I felt I couldn't allow us to just "enjoy our time together." It wasn't that I couldn't watch her body deteriorate, though that was admittedly, extremely painful for me. It was because I loved her enough to put my own feelings aside to free her from her body so that she could be in spirit. I believe that at the Rainbow Bridge, she could run and be who she was when her body was healthy; in other words, she could be herself again.

I wanted Frida to know that she was "truly loved" by her humans and the animal companions that she lived with under our roof. "Truly loved" was engraved on her gravestone.

At her end, Frida Rhea was so disoriented that she was in a state of limbo. When she died, I believe she felt great warmth from my holding her. When it was time for her to go, I finally accepted it.

I remember her spirit. Frida would dance when she got excited. I will always feel her presence.

Frida Rhea came to us to give us a sense of grounded state, stability, and a focal point. Her life was about knowing one's purpose in life and feeling good about it. She came to be with us to give the other dogs a sense of self-worth. She helped the group come together and stay rooted. She was the epitome of calmness.

Frida's best friend was Obie, a Black Labrador Retriever. He gave her comfort. Frida's final message to Obie was, "You are free to be whoever you want to be. You've been given the freedom to be yourself." Relax, my friend.

Best friends, Obie the Protector

Illness doesn't define Frida. When she was sick, she felt locked up and unable to move, her body had a sensation of being frozen, not cold, but not being able to move about. Now she gives it little attention. She was healed through death and is in wellness now at the Rainbow Bridge.

I must come to peace with her passing. Frida Rhea is already there.

The Story of Obie

I volunteered to groom dogs who needed medicated baths due to various skin conditions, at a local sanctuary. That's where I met Obie.

Obie at 12 years old was clearly a senior dog. He was graying around the muzzle and had "oil sacs" hanging from his legs. Not painful, but more a cosmetic issue, in a funny way it made him look prehistoric.

As the weeks of grooming passed, Obie and I grew closer. On grooming day, Obie would prance to the grooming room. End of the day, I came home with Obie stories for my husband. I couldn't stop talking about him and thought about him constantly during the week. My husband and I found ourselves spending a lot of time discussing adopting Obie, but had to consider all our questions: Could we manage another dog? Could we afford extra veterinary costs? Do we have room in the house? How would another dog change our household schedule? The day came when it was obvious that Obie was coming home. It felt right. He needed to be with us.

More importantly, we needed him. People don't really adopt animals, they adopt you, and Obie adopted us.

The first day with Obie was remarkable. He fit right in to our household. When evening came, Obie laid down in his bed. I leaned over him to give him a night kiss; he lifted his head and snapped at me. I realized that Obie never had a kiss before going to bed for the night, something I would have never thought of but made sense. The days afterwards, Obie looked for his night kiss, knowing it meant something good and was not a threat.

At Obie's age, we sacrificed cute for character, naïve for wise, baby fur and baby teeth for a graying muzzle and some needed dental work. However, we also had a dog who, after living in an outdoor pen for almost 12 years, was perfectly house-trained. Obie wanted to live in a house, be a part of a family, and seemed to know what do to and when to do it. He loved his orthopedic bed, his blanket and his new blue bowls. He was full of fun, had a lot of personality, was very affectionate and wanted to be loved and accepted.

Middle-aged and senior dogs have much to offer in the way of love and companionship. They are smart and do not require the training a younger animal might. There are no secrets about what they'll look like when they grow up. Do not deny yourself the experience of sharing your life with an older animal that someone else might turn their back on because of age. The rewards of owning a senior pet far outweigh the signs of aging.

Obie didn't mind how old I was, so I didn't mind how old he was. The time that I had with Obie was one of the richest, most rewarding experiences of my life because, as anyone who has ever owned a senior animal will understand, love knows no age.

My husband and I knew we wouldn't have Obie forever—we humans outlive our animal companions. In Obie's case, our time with him was shortened because we met him in the autumn of his life. But we knew whatever time we had with Obie, our time with him would be more rewarding and fulfilling than it would be without Obie.

In Obie's last days, he became incontinent and was on medications. He had urgency; he got up from sleep, or had the sensation to urinate, and sometimes could make it as far as the front door to go outside. He drank a lot of water and urinated frequently. Obie sometimes defecated in his bed. Again, he would try to make it to the front door to go outside, but sometimes could not and would have an accident in the house.

Obie had a difficult time maintaining a regular eating schedule. He would often not want to eat in the morning, but rather at noontime. He sometimes would not eat in the evening at feeding time but would want to eat late in the evening. We tried to keep him to a normal feeding schedule so that his urination/defecation times were more normal for our household. Though we tried to hold him to a normal feeding schedule, when Obie was hungry, he was very cranky!

Obie seemed to otherwise be mentally alert. I didn't think that his problem was cognitive. His sense of timing seemed to be "off" and therefore part the problem, but otherwise he was responsive and seems to know what is going on around him.

I believe Obie understood that he had something inside which was uncomfortable and sensed that this intrusion that caused his discomfort and failing. I believe he was saddened, knowing it would bring about the end of his physical being.

Every soul, at least the souls of the animal world, have an understanding and an acceptance of moving from the physical body to spirit. It is a beautiful gift. It is a rebirth, but it is also heart-wrenching to leave the ones we love behind. Animals are no different from humans in that regard. They struggle through the pain and discomfort of their failing bodies while holding on to the love of their humans, cherishing each moment. It is a period of thankfulness and honor of the wonderful union of human and animal. When it is their time to leave us, we give them the gift of letting go. "Hold my head and I'll take your love with me. That's what I want."

Obie had a blessed, glorious life. He loved me and thanked me through loving eyes. I always smile when I think of Obie. I'll always remember how we've touched each other's lives. I will always know that I only need to think of Obie and he will be by my side.

Every day of my life was richer because Obie was a part of it.

As Taught by the Animals

Learn from the animals. They have so much to teach us about their lives and ours. Don't miss this opportunity to personally grow and expand. The animals would have it no other way.

I continue to be amazed at the emotional sharing that goes on between my animals and me; when they feel good, I feel good; when they are happy, I'm happy. I feel such positive energy when I'm doing something for my animals, as opposed to doing something for myself.

Animals make me aware of moods and emotions that humans experience and animals don't, even thoughts of suicide, pity, and the futility of worry.

Animals can change my mood when I'm sad, because when they are with me, I feel the support they give. They are a constant reminder that fears and negativity can be overcome, or at least, let go. By their example, I am reminded that past traumas can be put behind. They can accept less than perfect circumstances through endurance and perseverance. Animals do not dwell on the past, but live in appreciation of the moment, appreciation of the day. By watching their purity, I am reminded of the elements of my behaviors and attitudes that still need refinement. I can be motivated to go to work when I really don't feel like it, to provide for my animals.

Power is a strength-evoking word. Animals help me to see the power of my maternal instinct as protector and caregiver. When I massage or pet an animal, I experience the power of healing that I hold in my hands through touch, for both the animal and me. I have experienced the power of small gestures, a lick of the hand, the warmth of a beloved pet lying next to me, stroking their fur, looking into deep, loving eyes, companionship. Through my relationship with animals, I've come to know the power of positive energy. I wouldn't want to live in a house without my animals, knowing the energy that they bring to the environment, and the emptiness that exists without them. To my way of thinking, all of this is a tribute to the power of the human-animal bond.

Animals teach us about life, more than we would know without their example. They show us the importance of establishing a balance between activity and rest to properly care for oneself. Routine, schedules, consistency and clarity are good things because they provide a sense of security and stability. They give us something to count on, in a world that can be very fragile. My close relationship with the animals in my life helps me to keep my priorities straight. I see that animals appreciate their small achievements, like watching an older dog fetch a ball, even if rolled along the floor rather than having it thrown.

I'm reminded that learning really can be lifelong, in an environment that offers mental stimulation and challenge.

Animals take pleasure in the simple things—food, water, a comfortable bed, a favorite activity, lying in the sun. They teach of the simplification of life, and the importance of basics.

I watch their highly developed skills of observation and I aspire to achieve their greater awareness and sensitivity. My animals teach me, by example, that choices are driven by who we are: our strengths, skills, and needs. Animals bring me to a better, more genuine understanding of life and death, and the transition between the two. Life is to be accepted as a continuum of stages, inevitably moving towards death.

Animals help us grow beyond physical, emotional, and behavioral issues. They are role models of patience; animals must sometimes wait for long periods of time for abuses to end, to find a home. They demonstrate forgiveness; my animals forgive me for my shortcomings every day. Animals are consistent; they have no sides to them, they are who they are. Through my animals I learn about trust; animals have taught me that trust is a precious gift someone has given to you. To respect trust, I have to try to be a person worthy of it. Sacrifice can feel good and be fulfilling; there are times when I am called upon to make sacrifices for my animals. Animals have taught me the true meaning of loyalty and devotion, as well as to hold these qualities in high regard. Spiritually, my animals make me feel nearer to God.

Animals give us unconditional love; giving to others without expecting anything in return. They teach me that responsibility is not life limiting; it can free a part of you that seeks expression. The French author Antoine de St. Exupery wrote, "We are responsible for what we tame."

I learn the meaning of family when I sense the warmth that the animals bring to the house, as opposed to the coldness I feel when they are not in the house.

I'm reminded of the many ways of communicating that do not involve speaking. Words are not always the only way, or the best way, to communicate. I appreciate every day for the opportunity to spend it with those I love, never taking time shared for granted. I come to understand what is involved in building a relationship; the day by day experiences of eating together, sleeping together, playing together, resting together. What makes a quality relationship is the time and attention spent each day, every day. Again, in the words of St. Exupery, "It is the time spent with your rose that makes it your rose." I don't question the importance of close relationships in one's life, I live that experience each day.

When humans and animals care for each other, it makes for a special balance in nature. Animals are children who never grow up. They teach me to care for something today while helping to create their tomorrow.

What is Animal Hospice?

Comforting an animal through the last days of their life brings great sorrow. Knowing that you did all you could, be it animal or human, reminds us of how fragile life really is. Your animal companion knows that you were there for them and now, watches over you from above.

The goal of animal hospice is to provide comfort, dignity, and a sense of peace to animals reaching the end of their natural lives. The focus of care is on sustaining the highest quality of life for whatever time remains.

The animal hospice movement is modeled after hospice services for humans. To understand hospice, one must grasp concepts of care giving, death and dying, and appreciate the rewards inherent in involving oneself in end of life issues. The intent is not to wallow in morbidity or evoke feelings of pity (the animals wouldn't want that), but rather to celebrate life. I hope that one day companion animals will be valued and granted worth, regardless of age or condition.

Animal hospice is a system of support for owners who have the physical and mental strength to care for their companions during the most difficult of life's passages. It provides compassionate care and comfort to both owner and beloved pet. Hospice services complement veterinary care and intervention. Hospice aids animals making an important journey. Their owners, who know them best, are in the best position to ease that transition. As the owners of senior animals know, dying is part of the experience of owning an older pet.

Hospice may be short-term or continue over a longer period. To make it work, owners must be willing to devote time and energy, and to accept the interruption to their normal schedule. The hours spent with an animal during the last days of its life can be an enriching experience for owner and pet. Hospice care gives families more time with an aging pet and helps them adjust to approaching death. It strengthens the bond between owner and pet and helps prepare the owner for the loss of a special companion. Hospice care allows an aging pet to enjoy the last days of life in familiar surroundings, in the company of loved ones.

This process takes a lot of energy; physical energy certainly, but also emotional and psychic energy, at a time when you will be preparing to experience the sadness of overwhelming loss. The final days are the time to spend with your beloved and devoted pet and help them cross the "Rainbow Bridge" to remember good times and build new memories together, to make this transition a peaceful one.

Though hospice is an alternative to premature euthanasia, it can also offer support in decision making when the quality of life can no longer be assured, and euthanasia must be considered.

Senior and Hospice Animals

As we observe the aging process in our beloved pets, it may remind us that we too, are growing older. Depending on how we view aging, we might see those changes as a natural part of life or reject what we see as something of which we'd rather not be reminded. Accepting that are pets will grow older as we will, appreciating that every stage of life holds something of value and worth, may help us accept the natural changes that come with aging. My hope is that we will move away from being a youth-oriented culture and come to appreciate life in its entirety.

We are all aging, and animals change over time. As we observe changes, some of those changes will bring us joy; some cause us pain. As animals age, physical changes may be sudden or gradual. They will experience good days and bad days. They may suffer ailments that will heal on their own, given a day or two, and some which will require veterinary intervention. You may observe drastic changes, or they may be so subtle that they are hardly noticeable. The effects on the animal may be profound, or so minute that they draw no concern. The change may be a one-time occurrence or may recur over time.

As animals age, they may experience physical ailments that cause them to feel discomfort. They may become frustrated with their own aging process. They might not hear as well as in younger years, their sight may be impaired, they may feel physically vulnerable when in the company of younger animals. They may have aches that they did not have before, or soreness in their joints and muscles. Be patient with your pet's changing moods and gradual decline. Your pet may become grumpy sometimes—it's not their fault!

Perhaps your pet's ailments cause you to react with impatience. This is a time that challenges you to develop patience with what is a natural process. The humans who share their lives with these amazing animals may be motivated to act immediately, when the correct course advises, "wait and see." Prepare to see changes.

Kate's Scars Touched Marie's Heart

It's just what you don't want to see while driving down a country road. The motorist ahead of you purposely swerves to hit a Beagle rambling along the road. The Beagle, panic stricken, dashed to avoid the oncoming vehicle. The car's tire bumps the dog, throwing her across the paved road. She skids along the hard surface, rolling most of the way, now seriously injured. The car keeps going, as you stop by the side of the road and proceed to call animal control. They arrive and take the animal to the local shelter.

The shelter had been cited by the state veterinarian for chipped and peeling paint. A deadline was put in place for the shelter to repaint, or it would be closed by the state veterinarian. A neighboring county offered to house all the dogs at the shelter until the painting was completed. Their animal control officers came to the shelter to assess the animal population. They came upon the injured dog and stood silent. They went on to explain to the shelter director that they were going to euthanize "Kate" because she was unadoptable given her age and injuries. Kate had already been accepted into our rescue, but it really didn't matter. At that moment, her fate had been decided.

Kate wore huge scars on her face, but particularly on her sides and back. Those scars covered at least a four to six-inch area, healing, but leaving an area of raw, browned skin, which would never grow hair.

The shelter director hurriedly called one of my board members to transport Kate to our rescue. I wasn't expecting company when I saw my board member's car come up our driveway, but went out to meet her, wondering to what I could attribute her arrival. Kate was in the back seat of her car, scared and bewildered, but safely delivered to our rescue.

At adoption events, everyone agreed that she had a great personality, but no one made a commitment to adopt her. One day I received an inquiry about Kate that came with a completed adoption application. I read it over in detail, concentrating on every point. It was the application from heaven, the application every rescuer wants to receive, and a home visit was arranged.

The volunteer who did the home visit came back to us with accolades for this potential adopter. "Marie's house is a wonderful place. The woman has owned Beagles for fifty years and is super nice. Yes, I highly approve this placement!"

The excitement in anticipation of Kate's arrival from Marie's voice was contagious. I arranged Kate's transport through volunteers in our area, put together her "go bag" full of information, freebies, toys and a leash that matched her collar.

Today I feel like Marie and I are old friends, bonded together by a road scarred Beagle, sweetness personified.

Why Should I Trust You? The Difficult Path

I have shared my life with senior and dying animals and found the experience to bring great peace and sense of satisfaction.

Depending on history, trusting can be difficult. Many issues are raised and brings up many experiences, past and present. The same can be said for animals. Patience is the key to helping them regain trust and build a forever bond. Not easy, by any means, but worth every moment spent. Our past influences our present but does not have to determine our future. With care, patience and understanding, the future can hold the promise of hope.

Maybe they're found wandering aimlessly down a road. Maybe they have been surrendered to a shelter or sanctuary. Maybe their owner goes into a nursing home, relocates, or for another reason cannot care for them, and abandons them. They are the animals we, the rescuers, see every day.

If they are lucky, they find space in a sanctuary or shelter. If they are luckier, they find themselves in a place that provides medical care. And if they are super lucky, they find their forever home.

Getting to that forever home can be a *difficult path*. The humans who are trying to place them often have limited knowledge of the animal's past. We, who rescue, want to give each of them every opportunity to be adopted by that perfect family. To accomplish that mission, the animal is expected to present well to others, both animals and humans; be smart, be housebroken, know as many commands as possible, and express affection freely—that's the animal that people want!

Now think of this story from the animal's perspective.

"You don't know me. You know what other people told you. You really don't know where I've been, or what I've been through. You say you'll make it better for me, better on whose terms? Why should I believe you? **Why should I trust *you*?**"

The animal that presents as shy, timid, moody, anxious, or even somewhat aggressive may have trust issues with humans. That path to find a forever home becomes more difficult when an animal has trust issues to work through. They may not gush with enthusiasm when a human walk up to them. They may not want to be petted. They may not show much desire to be affectionate at all. They may cringe or panic when approached. Maybe they freeze without even the slightest wag of a tail. Those expressions of emotion are real, because they are expressed with total honesty.

It takes time to build trust and patience and understanding. It also takes a belief that every animal who presents in this way has the potential to become greater, to become a trusting animal, to develop a genuine bond with that special person who can connect with them. They need a special person who can bring the qualities of time, patience and understanding to the relationship.

We tend not to be a patient society and few of us have an

abundance of time. Our capacity to understand can only be found internally, in the quiet moments when we sit and ponder who we are. Can we meet the needs of the animals in our lives? Maybe you can sense their thoughts when you're with them, maybe it's just a sensation that you get when you look in their eyes, or your innate response to their body language.

I ask myself, "Am I strong enough in character to meet the challenge this animal has brought into my life?" The relationship is not one-sided. You don't just serve the animal in need—the animal also serves you.

Why this animal, why now? How will I grow by sharing my patience, time and understanding with this being? What lessons am I to learn by allowing this animal in my life, at this juncture? Where will our mutual journey lead us?

Answers, at first, are unknown. The answers come as you accept the challenge and walk down the *difficult path.*

Rascal and Wheezy

Wheezy and Rascal were put in a basement laundry room for six months, with people who threw in an open bag of dog food to them and left it. The basement was dark and cold. No attention, they fended for themselves, Wheezy, a Dachshund, eating her fair share of the food as a Dachshund will do, and Rascal eating the leftovers. Neglected, both medically and nutritionally, and certainly without the affection of humans, they survived, somehow, we will never know. Then, brought to the attention of a fellow rescuer, we were contacted. Yes, we can accept them. Yes, we will meet all their medical needs. Yes, we will give them a home to call their own if not adopted.

Adopted they were! Rascal, by an independent Yorkie rescuer, who simply said to us, "Humans have heart strokes as Rascal has had, living in the basement and there is physical rehabilitation that can be done. I know those exercises as I have studied them. Let me adopt him and I will start his rehabilitation, pronto." She drove five hours to our rescue to meet Rascal, adopted him and now, he had a forever home. But wait! The story is not over! This adopter took him to the local board walk, took him to the beach, took him to art galleries, and showed him a world he would never otherwise seen. She did physical rehabilitation exercises with him that helped him walk again and navigate a world he would have never otherwise known. In time, over months, Rascal eventually passed in a park with his dog mom at his side. What a wonderful life he lived, experiencing things he would have never known, with the ability to walk, smell, and feel in a way that were unique to him. Rascal lived a full life before his passing, which was quiet, silent, and gentle, with a dog mom who cared deeply about his well-being in this world and the afterlife.

As for Wheezy, she came to us as a 26 pounds Dachshund— well overweight! She was fully vetted and put on a strict diet. Taken to an adoption event she met the person who would become her forever dog mom. This lady knew that she'd have to keep her on a diet and keep working with her and work with her she did. Wheezy lost enough weight to come down to 14 pounds. Oh, those last two pounds were hard to lose as anyone who has ever been on a diet will understand. Today, Wheezy has lost weight, been to Michigan, swimming, on the beach, and enjoying life. What a vacation! She lives in Charlottesville and has a life full of wonder and enjoyment with a woman and her fiancé who love her.

Rascal and Wheezy, when they came to us

*Wheezy on vacation
with her new mom*

*Rascal at the beach,
living the good life*

When They Fall Ill

Humans who have animal companions suffer as they worry about illness and aging, let alone the time when it comes to let them go. The grief for some becomes unbearable. Each of us grieves in our own way. My response to these individuals is to find peace in knowing that you were given the ability to love, to feel, and to grieve. I have spoken to hundreds of people who felt lost after losing an animal companion, with no one close to them who understood their grief. Peace comes in knowing that there are people who understand, who care, and who have had the same experience and moved through stages of grief. Be kind to yourself and if it is appropriate for you, make room in your heart for another animal friend. There are so many who need you. You'll know instinctively when the time is right.

You want to believe it is just going to be a singular event —your pet probably just ate some grass that didn't agree with her. Or maybe, she's just having an "off" day, as sometimes happens to humans. But after the second or third bout of lethargy, or vomiting, or diarrhea, you realize that your pet is more seriously ill.

A pet's illness can require you to do extensive housecleaning, as well as providing direct care, nursing, medication administration, and rearrangement of your normal routine. It's time consuming and energy draining. If you've ever experienced a sleepless night under these circumstances, or several sleepless nights, you know for yourself the toll it can take on your mental, physical, and emotional resources. You're exhausted during the other necessary activities that make up your day. Your patience wears thin and you become short tempered with people close to you. Still, you do what needs to be done lovingly, carefully, and attentively because the feelings that you have for your pet are so strong, so deep and connected that you just want to see your pet well again.

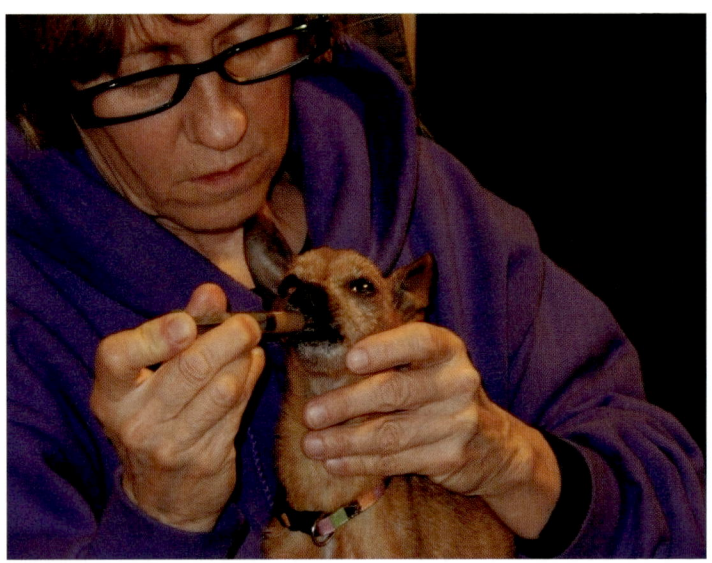

Giving a special feeding

You worry when recovery will come. Perhaps your pet does recover in a short time. Other times, a trip to the vet is needed. A trip to the vet can bring a sigh of relief and a quick cure; other times, not so.

You anticipate with worry and fear what will happen next. Will it be good news or bad? The thought of the potential expense can be daunting. If a second trip to the vet becomes necessary, you may be discouraged and agitated. Lastly, you may blame yourself for some level of negligence, imagined or otherwise. What could be worse than being a bad pet parent?

With senior pets, their limitations are always present in our minds. Will this be the end—the final illness? Or perhaps the repercussions will be so great that they will recover compromised by their illness with lasting conditions that will require on-going treatment? Do they have the strength and the will to battle what weakens them physically?

Usually, given time and perseverance, you see the gradual signs of recovery that give you the strength to keep going, bringing you closer to seeing the healthy glow of your pet again. You quickly forget your exhaustion, your strained emotions, and find the will to move forward.

There are other times when euthanasia is the most humane way to let our pet companions go, when there is no hope of improving their quality of life. When the situation allows, a peaceful passing may be the most we can hope for, the gift of eternal rest.

Satin Comes Home!

There was a dog in the orchard across the road, lost and quite pregnant. Taffy gave birth to five puppies, all of whom were adopted except for one. The last, unadopted puppy was named Satin, for her soft, furry, coat.

When Satin was 13 years old, she had never lived in a private home. She had a place to stay at a sanctuary for life, if need be, with people who worked with her and gave her love. Satin got along with other dogs and cats and loved everyone. I decided to open my home to her. Satin came to my home and adjusted to her surroundings. It speaks to so many dogs in shelters and sanctuaries, who, once adopted, make a beautiful transition.

It was the perfect day for a new adoption, because my husband and I would be home over the next few days to observe Satin closely. Satin walked to my car, I placed her in the passenger side and off we went!

I wanted Satin to stay separate from the other dogs at first, so she could gradually get to know the smells and sounds of our home without being intimidated by the other dogs.

That evening, a storm was approaching. In the distance, there was thunder and lightning. We turned on a floor fan and the television as a distraction from the sounds of the storm. The storm was brief, and Satin was fine.

We offered Satin a light supper, but she was not interested. By the next morning, I expected she would feel more comfortable in her new surroundings and be ready to eat. I brushed and combed Satin. It was a great "bonding" activity for both owner and pet!

We took Satin out for walks every two hours. We went back and forth through the house and started introductions with the other dogs. It was obvious that Satin was getting along with everyone and the dogs were ready to accept her. Still, we kept meeting times short, moved slowly, and allowed the process to unfold gradually. There was no need to rush.

It was bedtime for everyone, and that included dogs. Bedtime is "treat time" at our house and we quickly learned that Satin loves treats!

We had no problems all day. Satin learned that if you go to the front door, someone will take you outside. That seemed kind of cool! The other dogs adjusted nicely to a new resident and Satin soaked up the attention from animals and humans alike.

Under careful supervision, we allowed Satin to explore the house even more. Everything was so new and different, she loved looking in every corner. She paced around the house, probably a little anxious, but settled down by the next day.

After work, I was delighted to see that Satin still has no accidents, knew to relieve herself outside, and decided to eat her full bowl of food. There were dog toys that the others left all over the house. The other dogs enjoyed having someone new with whom new to play. Satin was popular because Satin was fun!

As the days went by...

My husband and I made a commitment to Satin to be consistent and clear, loving and dedicated, and provide for her needs, physical and emotional. We knew that it would take time and energy for real bonding to happen and to help Satin understand the household routines. However long it takes, we would make this transition work!

Just because an animal has never had a home, it doesn't mean that the animal can't adjust to a new home and love it. Was it a difficult transition? Not to my mind. Do we consider this experience to be a success? Definitely!

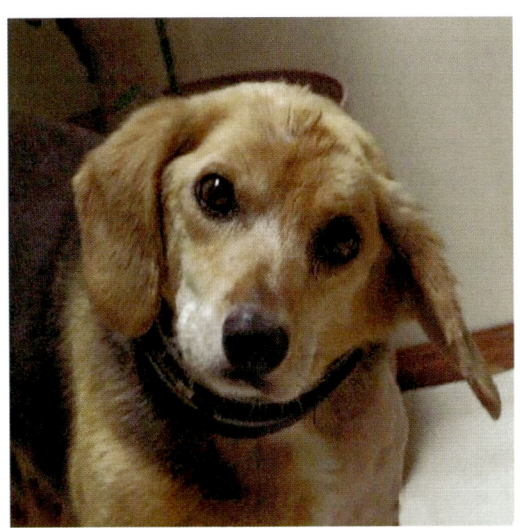

Satin, loved by her rescuers

What better satisfaction can one have than to know you gave a home to an animal that would not have known what it was to walk on carpeted floors, lay on a couch or in a chair, and see humans preparing dinner in a kitchen. Satin, at 13 years old, was still excited to learn about a television set, a vacuum cleaner, watch her humans do laundry, and participate as a family member in all the small everyday events that make a house, a home. Our "new" dog was older, but at least she would not leave this world without knowing the love of a family, both animal and human, and a home to call her own.

Memorializing our Beloved Pets

Expressions of grief are as individual as the people who seek our condolence. Some prefer to suffer in solitude. Others find comfort in sharing their memories and feelings of loss. Some remember their pets in private, while others find peace in a gathering of family and friends. For those that are not sure, I try to help them find what feels "right" to them. Together we identify ways of expressing their sorrow, to memorialize their memories of the pet they held so dear.

A favorite story of mine is that of Byron and his beloved Beagle, Matthew Shane, known to all as "Matt." Byron first saw Matt on a local television "spot" used for publicizing animals available for adoption. The Beagle puppy was at the Old Dominion Animal Hospital in Charlottesville for his initial vetting, but available there to be seen by members of the public who might be interested in pursuing his adoption. It was Byron who brought Matt home.

Upon Matt's passing, Byron chose to hold a memorial

service for his animal companion. I was honored to speak at the service. He was a wonderful Beagle, rescued and loved, on earth and beyond. Here is my tribute to Byron and Matt.

A Tribute to Matthew Shane Harris

I am much honored to be here, and more honored that Byron has asked me to speak. I have some thoughts that I want to share.

I view this last phase in Matt's life as the culmination of a life well lived, though I acknowledge that this is a time that is infused with sorrow and grief for those who have survived Matt. In the time I came to know Byron and Matt, these are things I saw, and why they both reminded me once again, of the power and the strength in the human-animal bond:

- Matt had a human who loved him dearly. There are millions of animals (and people for that matter) who die with no one to love them, no one to be with them, no one who cares. In that regard, Matt was very blessed.

- Matt had been very well cared for! I think of the homeless animals and people, the poverty stricken, the drug addicted. Of all the fates one could have, Byron, Matt landed very "soft" in your care and love.

- Byron, by your own description, Matt was able to bring out something very profoundly human in others. I think it may affect how you think about those close to you forever. It says so much for Matt.

- There have been times when I've thought, "Who will cry when I'm gone?" I think those thoughts are more common than not. Matt didn't have to wonder; Matt knew who would cry for him. This is a great tribute to you, Byron, and who you are.

- Animals die before humans. There are so many that die without any recognition of their lives. There are those that are abandoned, abused, or reach their maximum days at a kill shelter. Matt found Byron and never had to fear those endings. He knew security and warmth.

- Byron, you never gave up on Matt and Matt knew that. You called for help. You called me. You called a vet when he needed medical attention. I hope when I'm reaching the end that someone will be there for me. And if that person can't help me directly, I hope they'll call for help from others. Matt couldn't call for help himself. He needed you and you were there.

- It is a reality that many dogs suffer horrible fates. They don't have someone to think about honoring their lives, where they will spend their final resting days, to comfort their final hours. Matt had all that and more

- Matt meant so much to so many. You will probably never really know the joy he brought to others in even small ways, a simple greeting, and a wag of the tail.

- Byron, when Matt started to age, you didn't think of him as "some old Beagle." You didn't dump him because he started graying around the muzzle. I could see in your eyes, to you, Matt had always been the two-year-old you first adopted. Even as he aged and became ill, you didn't see his body as broken, though you grieved the thought of losing a dear friend. Now that his final passage has come, we know that you, as Matt's dad, will always see him as the dog you first saw on the TV, the dog you met at Old Dominion Animal Hospital, the one to whom you opened your home. You may be the only one who can see Matt with those eyes. Know that those are very special eyes, the eyes that don't see age, the eyes that remember the good times, and the eyes that acknowledge the worth, even in the body that was no longer willing.

Matt had a lot of positives going for him, and Byron, you do too.

Monty, the Survivor

Monty was left in a building with little or no food and not much care for about eight months. The house was dirty and awful. The person who contacted me was a sister in law of the person who owned him and knew his situation was deplorable. She worried every night, knowing that he was living in these conditions, but because her brother and the owner had divorced, it made communication very difficult. Our rescue was contacted and asked to accept Monty, which we did. He came to us emaciated with major medical issues. Other than needing vaccines and blood work, he was diabetic and needed pancreatic enzymes. Slowly, Monty put on weight. We had his glucose levels checked on multiple occasions, and we finally got his insulin dosage correct. The pancreatic enzymes helped immensely. Today. Monty is a healthy dog that will unfortunately probably never be adopted because his insulin and his pancreatic enzymes are costly. Not a problem! He can live with us if he has a quality of life, and we believe that will be for a very long time. Active, playful, gets along with other dogs and a true family member, Monty is a great dog. We wish others would see the greatness in him.

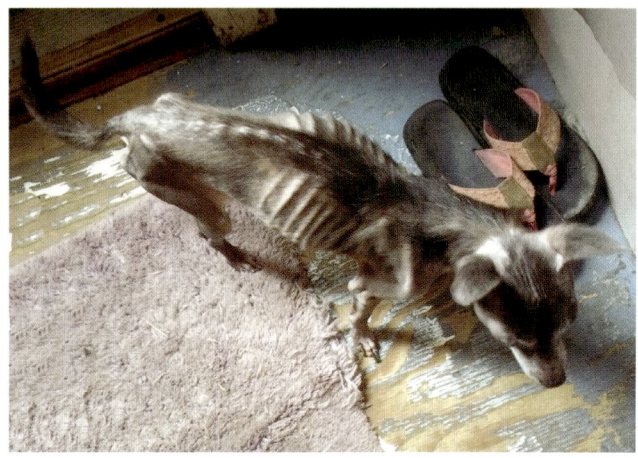

Monty when rescued

Monty, feeling better, looking handsome

Adopting an Older Dog

Puppies are cute. Seniors have soul.

There are lots of reasons older dogs become homeless. Some of them are: the death of a guardian, not enough time for the dog, change in work schedule, new baby, need to move to a place where dogs are not allowed, and kids going off to college, allergies, change in "lifestyle," or maybe a prospective spouse just doesn't like dogs.

If you have ever felt "not quite up to par" or remember the last time your heart was broken, you know how middle-aged or senior animals feel when they find themselves at an animal sanctuary or shelter.

By adopting an older dog, you'll make a statement about compassion and the value of life at all ages. Just as a puppy has his whole life in front of him, so does an older dog have *his* life in front of him. You can give that older dog the best years of his life while at the same time bringing a wonderful addition into your family. Older dogs are good at giving love. They are grateful for the second chance they've been given.

Older dogs usually have had some training, both in obedience and house manners. An older dog can be much easier to train than a puppy. Many rescued dogs were trained in their past; with a little encouragement it will come right back to them. The key to house training is not age, but your patience and consistency in training the loved one.

Older dogs have the same medical needs as younger dogs. Veterinary attention and medication are needed at all ages and may or may not be costlier for an older dog. The same can be said for humans. With a health assessment, you will know what age-related conditions are present and you can take appropriate measures to address them.

My senior dog doesn't mind how old I am, so I don't mind how old he/she is. The time that I have with them is one of the richest, most rewarding experiences of my life because, as anyone who has ever owned a senior animal will understand, love knows no age.

Older dogs are more settled. You know what you are getting because they have grown into their shape and personality. Older dogs can focus well because they've mellowed. They are calmer and quieter. They have learned what is expected of them. Older dogs know what "no" means, because if they hadn't, they would not have gotten to be "older dogs." They are easy to assess for behavior and temperament. Older dogs, especially those who have known it, appreciate love and attention and quickly learn what is expected of them to gain and keep that love and attention. The older dog is not trying to prove his dominance over humans and is ready to fit himself into your family "pack." They will do whatever is necessary to make that fit as comfortable as possible.

Maybe you are reluctant to adopt a senior dog because you fear that your time with your new best friend will be short, bringing that painful time of loss closer. But the privilege of loving a senior dog makes every single day special, as you and your companion share love, friendship, and a special relationship that grows stronger with the knowledge that you have given an older dog a second chance at life.

The love that grows from this knowledge is much stronger than the pain of eventual separation. Adopting an older dog is life-altering. You will gain a faithful companion. Senior dogs and senior people bring out the best in each other. Old dogs make great friends! You will have shared your life with a great spirit and that experience will profoundly affect your life for the better. Consider that there are never any guarantees about length of life with any dog. Quality of time together can matter a great deal more than quantity. The knowledge that you have changed the life of a single animal in need will fill you with both satisfaction and peace. You won't have to wonder if your efforts made a difference, you will know it.

Spend some time with senior animals. Even in a very short time, you won't think about how old the animals are, or what special needs they might have, but whether you are worthy of making a home for such a special animal companion. And be assured that you will be embarking on one of the most enriching, rewarding adventures of your life.

Moving Towards Spirit

Each day, we all move towards spirit.

When I was young and curious, but old enough to understand, I asked my mother questions about my birth. Let me say, that I don't think my birth was particularly different from any other birth, nor eventful from any aspect other than another new life brought into this world. My mother explained my birth in detail and was open to responding to my inquisitive nature.

Quite frankly, the more I heard, the more I couldn't believe that she lived through the experience, or that I did. Birth is, in its own way, traumatic. There is a side to it that is stressful, coupled by physical labor and discomfort. Yet, it is generally viewed as a blessing. It is a life event, a passage, a new beginning. The story left me with this impression: if I could live through my own birth, I am convinced that I can live through death.

If you are someone who has made peace with the thought of your eventual passing, this writing may not be relevant for you. However, it is my impression that as a society, many of us do not deal well addressing the subject of death, as applies to ourselves or our pets.

I have met people who accept their own birth as a natural passage without associating it with fear or trauma. We can speak of birth openly, brag about the new arrival, and receive reinforcement from those around us for doing so. Not so, with the issue of death. In our society, the subject of death is to be avoided, only spoken of when necessary, and associated with all that is unpleasant. Certainly, we grieve over the loss of a beloved pet—that's natural. But our reluctance as a society to accept aging and death as a natural process inhibits us from learning about the process of death, confronting our fears, and communicating our thoughts and feelings on the subject to others. Our beloved animal companions, whose lives are much shorter than our own, can suffer because of the negative attitudes' humans hold regarding death.

In my work with senior and hospice animals, I meet many people with aging animal companions, and even more animals that have been abandoned in what was to be their "golden" years. Our aging pets frequently remind us of our own aging process, the aging process we'd often rather avoid. As we watch our animal friend's muzzle grow gray, we look at ourselves in the mirror and more closely note our own fine lines of aging. Maybe it's their slower gait, or the eyesight that begins to fail, or the need for us to speak louder so that our pets can hear us, which brings the aging process home. Birth "happens" to us, but aging comes slowly, giving us way too much time to think about it, worry about it, and fret. If we have fears about death, those fears can intensify when we see the manifestations of age in our pets. Most of us are horrified when we hear of a senior pet being abandoned for a new puppy, or abandoned because they are growing old, or when needed medical care was cost-prohibitive. Yet, it happens all too often.

If we could ever become comfortable with the idea of our own passage, our own transition into spirit, how the world might change for the better. An elderly pet might not be in danger of becoming a "throw away," criticized for exhibiting to us the natural process of aging. Rather they would be exalted for allowing themselves to experience all the rich, glorious stages of life, including those that move us towards the end of life. We might come to appreciate aging in the same way our society seems to value all that represents youthfulness. Aging would be valued as the "crone" in the wise-woman tradition; she who possesses wisdom, brings experience, and views the world from a position of knowing.

I am growing older; it is inevitable. But as this happens, I will watch my senior animal companions and learn from them. I will be patient with their aging process and my own. I will see beauty in their eyes, look beyond the body that might not function as perfectly as in puppyhood or kittenhood, and see the spirit that will be with us, among us, long after the body has passed, having aged with grace.

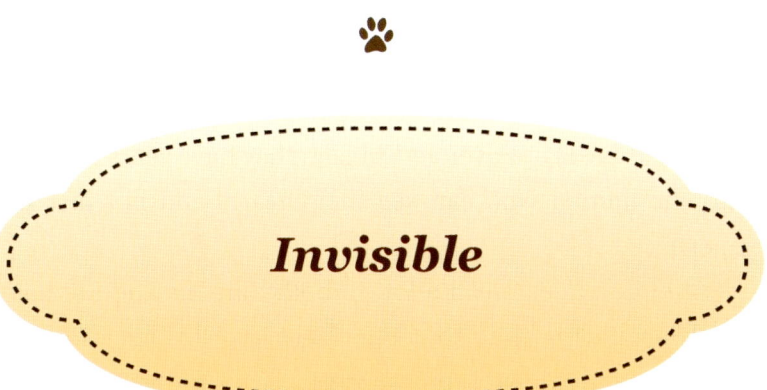

Invisible

For both humans and animals, aging can make us "invisible."

A friend of mine asked her 90-year-old mother what it was like to grow old. Her mother responded, "you become invisible." The theme resounded with me when I heard the story, growing older myself. As my hair grays and the years pass, I notice I get less attention, particularly from the opposite sex. The flirting stops, the loving gestures are no more. Yes, I'm reminded that I'm no longer seen as sexy, pretty, or attractive as an aging woman. I don't feel old! Yet, I've become invisible.

I see the same thing happen to my senior dogs. Everyone loves to hold puppies. People gravitate to younger dogs to stroke them and comment on how pretty they are, how cute, how playful. Those puppies sure enjoy a lot of attention! Like the aging human, the senior dogs become invisible. The more common comments are things like, "she is so sweet," "poor old dog," "oh, he's blind," "he doesn't hear well, does he?" The focus is on the signs of aging, the gray hairs, the sight and hearing that is waning, rather than the magnificent companion, the strengths he or she possesses, the love they give. Their life is not over yet! In fact, they have years to spend with the human who can see their hearts and not just the superficial.

Attention does mean a lot, to both humans and animals. Attention means that someone "sees" you, takes the time to notice you, talks to you, appreciate you for who you are, without judgment. Being recognized for having something to offer to someone else. It builds your ego, makes you feel worthwhile, desirable, boosts our self-esteem, and that gives us confidence. It also gives us recognition that we are part of this world, have a place, and others see us.

Beauty is not skin deep. It is much more than that. What is on the outside does not show what is on the inside. But what we react to is the external, and in the world of senior animals, too often, because the external shows the signs of a life lived, we reject what we see and turn to the younger animal who does not remind us of ourselves and our own aging process. Respect aging. For both animals and humans, don't let the aging process let us become "invisible."

Old Dog

Many senior animals languish at shelters with little hope of being adopted. Please consider adopting a senior. The rewards are great, and you'll know you gave an animal a chance to know what it is to have a family to call their own in their later years.

I only have one flaw—I'm aging. I want someone to take me home, just like my juniors. I'm basically good-natured. My tail wags, maybe a little slower than you'd like. Oh, my legs have their stiff days, and my colors aren't as brilliant as they once were, now that my hairs are mixed with gray. I wait in my pen for you to visit and when you do, I'm happy to see you approach. Maybe you just walk by me. Maybe you stop and say, "Poor old dog!" And maybe your eyes turn away, because I remind you that, you too, are aging every day.

When you walk by my pen without stopping, I know, as you do, I've lost my chance to show you how wonderful and majestic an animal I truly am. I've done nothing wrong; I just got older, as you do, one day at a time.

I don't know where the time went! Just yesterday, I could run and play for hours and jump so high! Now, I move more cautiously. My eyes and body movements aren't as coordinated as they once were. Still I love to have fun, if in a more subdued way. I want to experience new things and challenge my mind, while I am able. My jumps are measured in inches—the same jumps that were once measured in feet.

Don't pity me, because I don't pity myself! I've had good times and bad times in my life, just like you.

What time I have left, I'd like to spend with family who loves me. I wish I could keep you with me forever, but I can't, just as one day you'll have to leave your loved ones behind. Can't we just make the most of today?

Soften your eyes and look at me with the same excitement as if you were looking into much younger eyes. Spend some time with me and see beyond the signs of aging, see my heart, come to know my soul. I have so much to offer.

I wait in my pen, looking for a human companion to come along, hoping that you will stop by and stay with me awhile. Look beyond the superficial, look deeper and open your heart.

Take me home. We'll sit together and think profound thoughts. I'll lie next to you and support you when times seem bleak. We'll face life together, whatever time it is that we will share. When the time comes for us to part, I'll go with grace and watch over you from above.

Dog Mom

Parenting pets is a skill like any other—it requires learning and practice. Sometimes even the best pet parents need support. A support network of friends and family is essential as an outlet for expressing your joys and frustrations. Animal people will gladly listen to your pet stories and be genuinely interested in hearing more. You'll feel that you have someone who truly understands what you are experiencing with your pet, good days and bad. The more pets you own, the more useful a pet support network, because animal people understand other animal people. The ideal situation is to co-parent with another family member, as you will have a source of mutual support; to share information, offer condolence, and help with care giving tasks.

I'm a dog mom.

When I talk with excitement about the anticipation of a new arrival,

No one throws me a puppy shower.

When a new furry family member arrives home,

No one asks to see the pictures.

When my dog improves her behavior or does something cute,

No one asks or listens.

My dog doesn't sell Girl Scout cookies,
But I'm often asked to buy them from friends and colleagues.
My dog doesn't raise money for the band,
But it seems that all my friends' children do.
My dog isn't in a French class that's raising money to go
to Paris,
Though for such good causes, I'm often asked to contribute.

I seem to be needed to feed, clean up after, and medicate,
And travel to the vet's office on numerous occasions.
I have calendars of shots and check-ups to keep up with,
That requires me to be a master of time management.
I do laundry, clip nails, and maintain a regular bath schedule,
And still I am not considered a "mom" by some.

I'm a dog mom.
I give and get unconditional love.
My dogs cuddle and kiss and jump up and paw.
I can see eyes light up and tails wag.
Their nudges tell me I'm doing something right.

The personnel policy manual doesn't define me as a mom.
When my dogs need to go the vet, family sick time
doesn't cover.
When my dogs are sick, family leave time can't be used.
I use up my annual leave to be with them during their
dark hours.

Still I wouldn't choose to do anything differently;
It's my choice to be a dog mom.

I worry the same as a human mom,
I watch every move and change.
I want them all to be healthy and well,
And grow up to be popular with others.

My life is centered on my dogs.
I practice parenting daily.
When I feel weak, my animals make me strong,
Strengthening my sense of family.

I spend a lot of time at home
Loving up my dogs.
I enjoy traveling when I can,
But always look forward to walking through the front
door again
To be greeted by faces who love me.

The love of my animal child keeps me alive,
carrying me through the worst work day.
That love motivates me to survive
the stresses of everyday life.
All become manageable at the end of the day,
When I experience the calm and contentment of knowing
I'm mom; I make a home for us all.

I love as much as a human mom

And when my dog suffers, I hurt.
I've spent evenings lying next to my pets
Administering medication and nursing them through illness.
And when those final days present themselves,
I grieve a mother's grief,
I'm empty, lost, and in pain.

I'm a dog mom.
I'll buy the children of friends and family
bridal shower,
wedding,
graduation,
birthday,
and Christmas gifts,
Knowing that the recipient will never think of buying a gift for
my pooch,
Or even inquire about their age and health.
I'll ask how my friend's children did in school this semester
and be shown report cards
Knowing that no one will ask if my dog was able to attend
doggie manners class.

So, think about your childless friends,
And notice who they love.
Maybe it is a child with four legs, lots of hair and a wet nose,
And ask them,
"How is your dog?"

About Peaceful Passings Senior Animal Rescue

Our mission of Peaceful Passings is to save senior animals and, when appropriate, re-home them to loving families. Our vision is world where no animal must be euthanized based on age and/or medical challenge when a quality of life remains. Animals will live a better life when humans respect that all stages of an animal's healthful life are of value to society.

In 2002, Peaceful Passings began as a rescue for senior animals supported only by my husband and myself.

In 2009, the process was begun to apply for non-profit status to expand our service to more animals in need by making ourselves able to accept donations to support our work. When our Letter of Determination was received, Peaceful Passings was granted non-profit status as a 501c3, which allowed us to accept donations and expand our rescue.

Our outdoor shelters, for the larger dogs

Our web site was developed to offer the public information on caring for senior animals and as a resource on death, dying, and grief issues. Many people were paying for their veterinarians for this information, which was knowledge well known to those of us who had volunteered in shelters and worked with senior animals for many years. Our thought was to make this information available to the public, so when people took their animals to a veterinarian, they would be able to apply their financial resources towards addressing their individual animal's medical needs.

Peaceful Passings is an all-volunteer organization. We have a six-member Board of Directors. Peaceful Passings serves three populations; seniors dogs age seven and older, our hospice animals who will remain with us if they enjoy a quality of life, and our special needs seniors. To date, we have accepted animals into our rescue mostly from rural counties in Virginia.

About the Author

I am a dog and cat mom. The individual situations that our animals found themselves in were created by the humans with whom their life paths crossed. Those situations often included domestic violence, abandonment, abuse, and neglect. They arrived at our home needing medical attention and training to meet their behavioral needs.

Today they are happy, well-behaved family members who have found their "forever home."

I consider my work with animals to be a "calling." I believe our choices in life are driven by who we are; what we need to feel complete. In that respect, my choice to work with animals is driven by a need to advocate for a "voiceless" population, our animal companions. It is a personal and spiritual mission to serve the animals that have graciously chosen to share their lives with me. I have been a human companion to animals for over forty years. I am a person who cares deeply for the wellbeing of all animals and has found a special calling to work with senior and hospice animals. The insight that I bring to the mission of animal service has been acquired over time and can be learned by anyone with the desire to do so.